Making Pictures
AMAZING ANIMALS

Materials

Start collecting materials to make the wonderful pictures in this book. You'll need paper and poster board, yarn and felt, sequins and beads, foil, glitter and paints, sponge, and fancy candy wrappers.

You can either make the pictures just the same as the ones in the book, or you can use the ideas to design your own. There are all sorts of exciting and unusual painting techniques for you to try out, too.

Designed by **Jane Warring**
Illustrations by **Lindy Norton**
Pictures made by **Karen Radford**
Photographs by **Peter Millard**

This edition © 1997 Thumbprint Books
Published by Rigby Interactive Library,
an imprint of Rigby Education
a division of Reed Elsevier, Inc.
500 Coventry Lane, Crystal Lake, IL 60014

Printed in Italy

00 99 98 97 96
10 9 8 7 6 5 4 3 2 1

Library of Congress Cataloging-in-Publication Data
King, Penny, 1963-
    Amazing animals / Penny King and Clare Roundhill.
       p.   cm. -- (Making pictures)
    Includes index.
    Summary: Gives directions for creating collages featuring various
kinds of animals.
    ISBN 1-57572-192-9 (lib.bdg.)
    1. Collage--Juvenile literature. 2. Animals in art--Juvenile
literature. (1. Collage. 2. Animals in art. 3. Handicraft.)
I. Roundhill, Clare, 1964-   . II. Title. III. Series: King,
Penny, 1963-   Making pictures.
TT910.K56 1997
702'.8'12--DC21

96-53241
CIP
AC

Making Pictures
AMAZING ANIMALS

Penny King and Clare Roundhill

Contents

A Crazy Caterpillar

Make this crazy caterpillar out of red and green felt or any other bright fabric.

To make the picture extra cool, give it a fingerprint border (see paint tip).

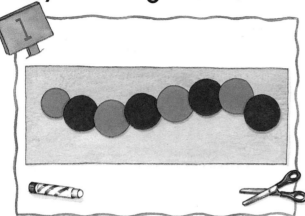

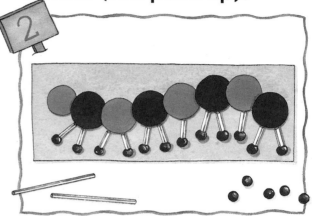

Cut out eight felt circles. Overlap and glue them on the yellow poster board.

Cut the straws into 12 short legs. Glue them to the body. Stick on shiny red bead boots.

PAINT TIP
Dip your finger into red paint. Press it onto the yellow poster board. Dip your middle finger into green paint. Make a print next to the red one. Repeat.

Make the antennae from strips of folded paper and glue them on. Stick beads on the tips.

Decorate the caterpillar's body with paper stars. Glue on a paper mouth and sequin eyes.

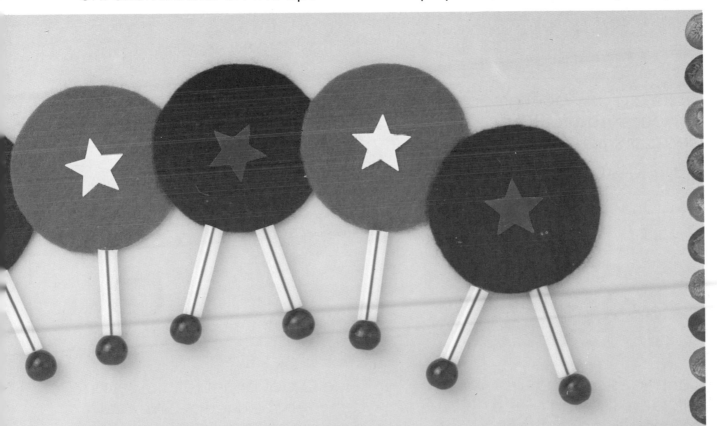

7

Spring Sheep

These fluffy sheep would make a good card to welcome spring. If you can find some small cotton balls, that is even better for making their bodies than large ones. Put the sheep in a grassy field full of spring flowers.

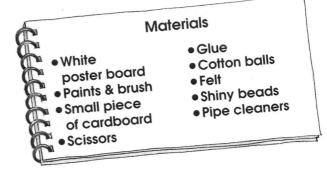

Materials
- White poster board
- Paints & brush
- Small piece of cardboard
- Scissors
- Glue
- Cotton balls
- Felt
- Shiny beads
- Pipe cleaners

Make a grassy background for your sheep to graze on (see paint tip). Let it dry.

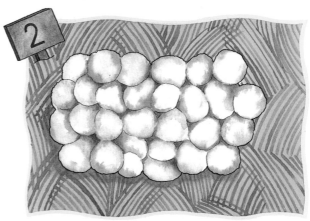

For each sheep's body, glue small cotton balls close together on the grassy field.

Cut heads and legs from black felt. Glue them in place. Stick on shiny beads for their eyes.

Glue lots of bright felt flowers in between the sheep. Give them pipe cleaner stalks and leaves.

9

Contented Cats

Why not make these two soft, furry, yarn cats sitting on top of a garden wall?

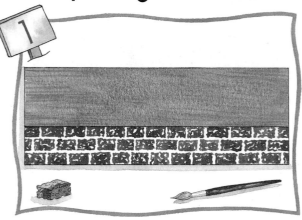

Print bricks along the bottom of the board (see paint tip). Paint a pale blue sky above it.

Add some bright yellow tissue flowers to give your picture extra color.

Cut cat shapes out of black or brown board. Glue yarn in lines or spirals all over them.

PAINT TIP
Cut a small rectangle out of sponge. Soak it in water and then squeeze it dry. Press it lightly in brown paint. Starting at the bottom left-hand corner of the white poster board, print rows of bricks, leaving a small space between each one.

Materials

- Sponge
- Scissors
- Old dish
- White, brown, and black poster board
- Paints & brush
- Scraps of yarn
- Glue
- Pink felt
- Beads
- Tissue paper

3

Add pink felt noses, yarn whiskers, and bead eyes. Then glue the cats on top of the wall.

4

Glue on flowers made from circles of yellow tissue with black centers. Add twisted tissue stalks.

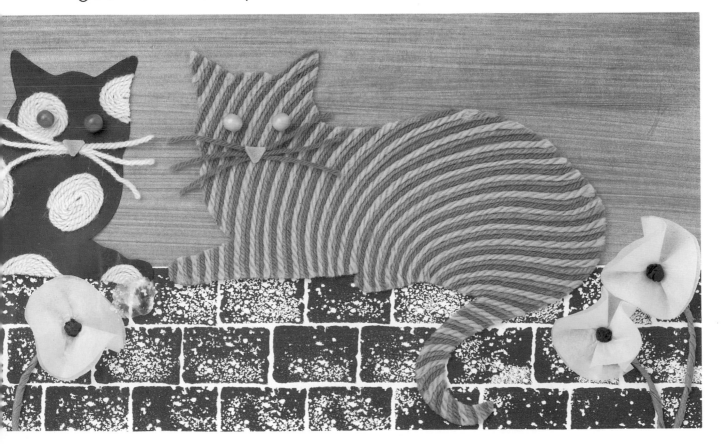

11

A Proud Peacock

Look in a sewing basket for scraps of patterned fabric to make this peacock with a magnificent tail. Use lots of different colors for the feathers. To make it look really proud, outline it with gold glitter, standing on a grassy background.

Materials

- Stiff white poster board & crayons
- Paints & brush
- Blue and green fabric scraps
- Felt
- Scissors & glue
- Red sequins
- Gold paper
- Red and gold pipe cleaners
- Gold glitter

Make a grassy background on the poster board for your peacock (see paint tip).

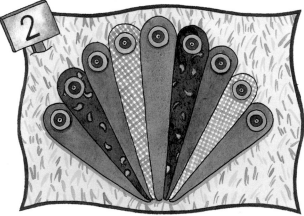

Overlap and glue fabric tail feathers onto the background. Add felt and sequin "eyes."

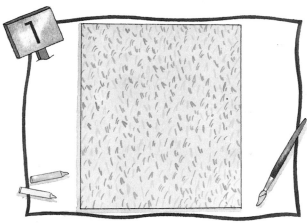

Cut out a blue fabric head and body. Glue it over the feathers. Glue on red pipe-cleaner feet.

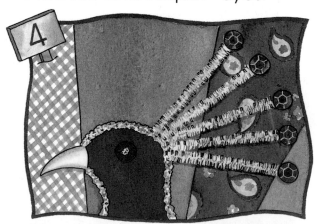

Give the peacock a gold beak, sequin eye, and head feathers made of glittery pipe cleaners.

PAINT TIP
Use crayons to draw short
blades of grass in yellow
and different shades of
green all over the white
poster board. Brush a coat
of watery green paint on
top. Let it dry.

13

A Dangerous Dragon

Turn a cardboard tube, yogurt container, and egg cartons into a dragon.

Paint it green and then decorate it with button eyes and beads or candy.

Paint the egg cartons (see paint tip), yogurt container, and tube for the head and body.

Cut tissue strips. Snip one edge to make a fringe. Tape them to the boxes and container.

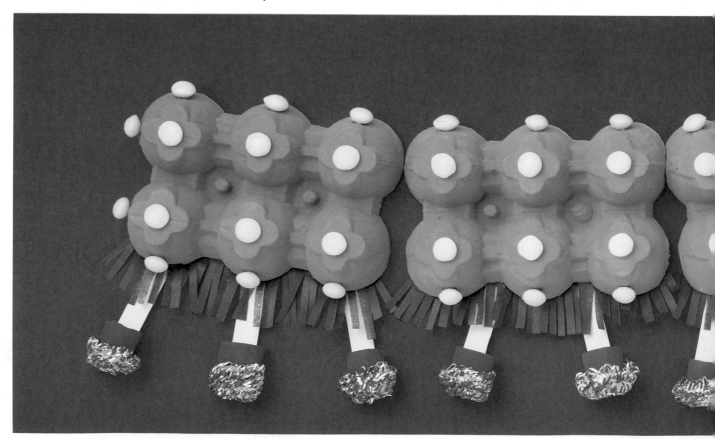

Materials

- 3 egg cartons
- Cardboard tube
- Yogurt container
- Paints & brush
- Tissue paper
- Scissors
- Glue & tape
- Pipe cleaners
- Buttons & beads
- Red poster board
- Chicken frills

3

Make eyes from pipe cleaners and buttons. Poke them through holes in the container.

4

Glue the dragon onto the board. Add paper legs, chicken frill feet, tissue flames, and spots.

15

A Zippy Zebra

Use strips of torn newspaper and magazine pages to create this amazing zebra galloping through the African grasslands. Trace a small plate onto white poster board or paper to make the full moon, and fill the sky with sparkling stars.

Materials

- White paper
- Plate
- Pencil & scissors
- Paints & brush
- Silver glitter
- Glue
- Black poster board
- Newspaper and old magazines
- Silver foil
- Sticky silver stars

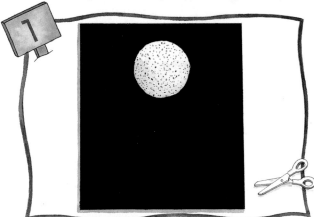

1. Cut out the moon and paint it (see paint tip). Glue it onto the black poster board.

Draw a zebra on newspaper. Glue on dark stripes torn from old magazines. Cut it out.

3. Glue the zebra onto the card. Tear newspaper grass strips and glue them across the picture.

4. Cut out silver foil stars. Glue them all over the sky along with some ready-made sticky stars.

PAINT TIP
To make gray paint, mix a dab of black into a large spot of white. Starting at the center of the moon, paint around in a spiral. Sprinkle glitter on while the paint is still wet, to make it glisten.

17

Darting Dragonflies

Dainty dragonflies, dancing and darting over a pond, make a wonderful picture.

Use the candle and paint for the water. Glue on beautiful dragonflies.

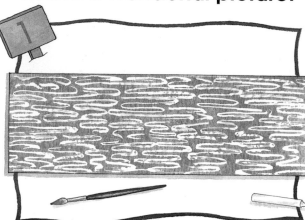

Paint a watery blue and white background for your picture (see paint tip). Let it dry.

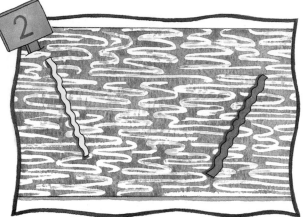

Cut a length of ric-rac for each dragonfly's body. Glue them at angles onto the water.

Materials

- White & colored poster board
- White candle
- Paint & brush
- Colored ric-rac
- Scissors
- Colored glitter
- Glue
- Paper doilies
- Candy wrappers
- Sequins
- Pipe cleaners

Cut out candy wrapper wings. Glue them in place and highlight with glitter. Add sequin eyes.

Cut out board and pipe cleaner bullrushes and tall green reeds. Glue them at the water's edge.

A Rugged Reindeer

Create a really different picture of a handsome reindeer made out of lots of tiny crumpled tissue balls. Give it big handprint antlers and a bright red nose. Set it against a background of sparkling snow and ice.

Materials

- Brown paint
- Paintbrush
- White paper
- Scissors
- White poster board
- Glue
- Sugar or salt
- Silver glitter
- Pencil
- Brown, red, and blue tissue paper

1

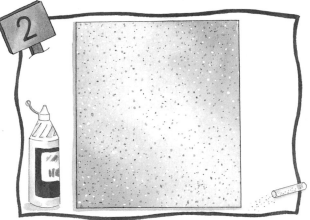

Make antlers with handprints (see paint tip). Let them dry before you cut them out.

2

Cover the poster board with glue. Sprinkle sugar and glitter on top. Shake off any extra.

3

Crumple small pieces of brown tissue into balls. Glue them down to make an outline of the head.

4

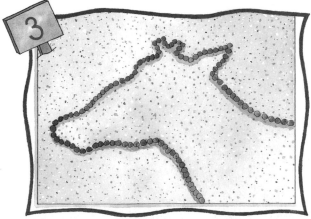

Fill in the head. Use blue for the eyes and red for the nose. Glue the antlers on top of the head.

PAINT TIP
Paint your left hand brown.
Press it down on some white
paper, with your fingers
spread out, to make a
handprint. Then paint your
right hand and make
another handprint.

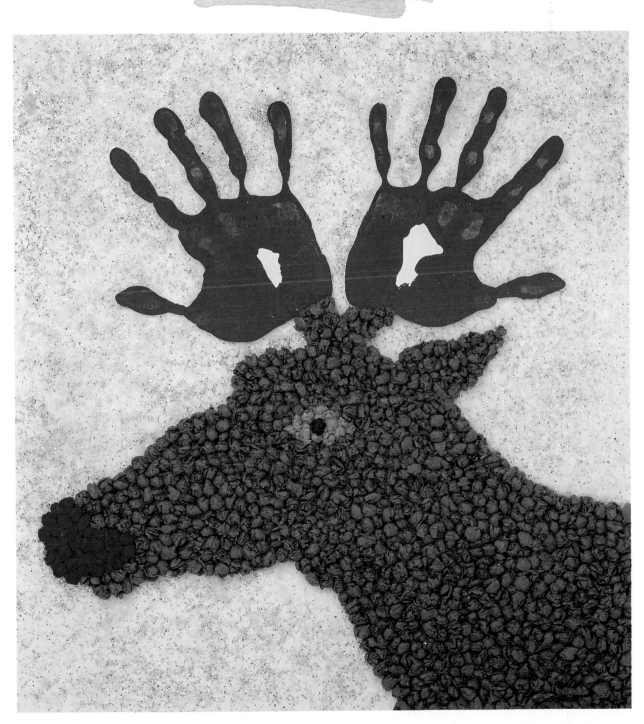

21

Funny Frogs

These croaking frogs sitting on lily pads and floating in a pond, make a funny picture.

Decorate the edge of the pond with green paper reeds and a glowing sun.

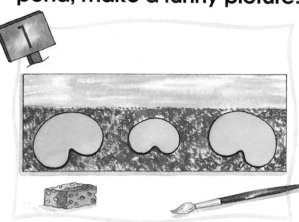

Paint the board (see paint tip). Glue on green paper lily pads, two big, and one small.

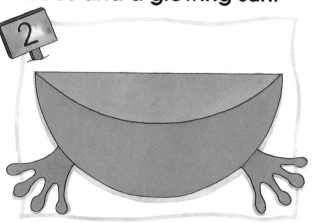

Cut dark green circles for the frogs. Fold each one in half. Glue on big green paper feet.

PAINT TIP
Thoroughly wet the white poster board all over with a damp sponge. Quickly brush strokes of light blue paint across the card. Let it dry. Dip a small sponge in darker blue paint. Dab it over the bottom half of the card to make ripples of water in a pond.

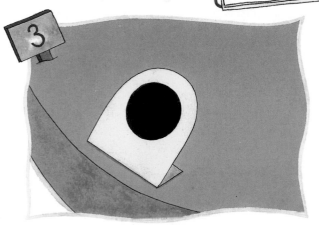

3 Make yellow paper eyes with black pupils. Bend and glue them to the frogs' heads.

4 Tape a pipe cleaner tongue inside each frog's mouth. Glue the frogs onto the lily pads.

23

A Perching Parrot

Create a crazy, colorful parrot, with rows and rows of bright tissue feathers. Give him a leafy green background and a real twig to perch on. Instead of using tissue feathers you could paint your parrot in bold colors.

1 Print a leafy background in different shades of green (see paint tip). Let it dry.

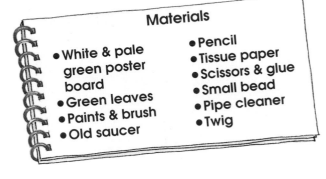

2 Draw a parrot on white board. Paint it and cut it out. Glue on rows of zig-zag tissue feathers.

3 Cut long tissue tail feathers in different colors. Glue them in place. Glue on a bead eye.

4 Wrap a pipe cleaner claw around a twig. Glue the twig and parrot onto the background.

Busy Bugs

Make a bright and busy picture of bugs, beetles, and crawly caterpillars.

Cut them out of felt and colorful paper. Glue them onto flowers and leaves.

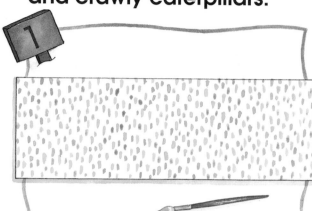

Paint a grassy background in shades of green on the white poster board (see paint tip).

Cut out colorful card leaves, flowers, and stalks. Glue them onto the grassy background.

Materials

- White & colored poster board
- Paints & brush
- Palette or plate
- Different colored felt
- Scissors
- Glue
- Pen
- Pipe cleaners
- Beads
- Shiny paper

PAINT TIP
To make blades of grass, dip the tip of a paintbrush into green paint. Dab it with quick flicks over the poster board. Use different shades of green and spread them out.

3 Draw beetles, bees, caterpillars, and other crawling bugs on colored felt. Cut them out.

4 Glue them onto the plants. Add pipe cleaner antennae, bead eyes, spots, stripes, and wings.

27

Enormous Elephants

To make both elephants the same size, fold a big piece of white paper in half.

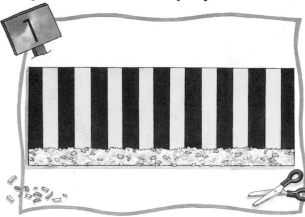

Glue red stripes on the yellow board. Spread glue at the bottom. Sprinkle on sawdust.

Draw an elephant on the top half. Then cut out both layers at the same time.

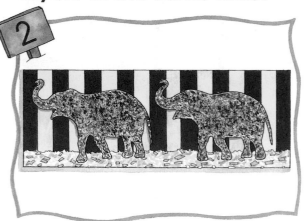

Glue the two elephants (see paint tip) on the poster board with their feet on the sawdust.

PAINT TIP

Draw an elephant and a separate ear shape on a big piece of white poster board. Cut them out. Wet a sponge and squeeze it dry. Dip it in gray paint. Dab it gently all over the elephants and their ears. Try the effect on a sheet of spare paper first.

Materials

- Yellow & white poster board
- Red paper
- Glue
- Sawdust
- Pencil
- Scissors
- Gray paint
- Small sponge
- Black beads
- Bright paper
- Sequins & glitter

Glue an ear on each elephant. Glue on a tusk and a black bead eye, as well.

Cut out bright paper blankets. Glue them on the elephants' backs. Add sequins and glitter.